not a guide to
Worthing

Wendy Hughes

The History Press

First published 2013

The History Press
The Mill, Brimscombe Port
Stroud, Gloucestershire, GL5 2QG
www.thehistorypress.co.uk

British Library Cataloguing in Publication Data.
A catalogue record for this book is available from the British Library.

ISBN 978 0 7524 7651 3

Typesetting and origination by The History Press
Printed in Great Britain

Coat of Arms

The borough's Coat of Arms represents the three main industries of the town up to the middle of the last century: fishing, seaside tourism, and market gardening.

*

The three silver herrings and the blue and silver bars on which the fish sit represent fishing and the seaside, and the horn of plenty overflowing with corn and fruit on a cloth of gold represent the riches gained from the earth.

*

The figure on the crest is probably Hygeia, goddess of health, holding a snake representing the powers of healing.

*

The motto, '*Ex terra copiam e mari salute*', means, 'From the land plenty and from the sea health'.

*

The arms were granted on 20 October 1919 and again on 25 November 1974, when the helmet and mantling, but not the crest, were added.

Contents

Worthing

Worthing – 'the place of *Worth* or *Wurtha's* people' derived from the Old English for valiant or noble one. *Ingas* – people of, shortened to 'ing' in modern times.

First recorded name: *Weoroinga*. By 1086 (Domesday Book): *Ordinges*.

The modern name was first documented in 1297.

Local legend states the town became known as *Wort* (weed) – *inge* (people) from a natural annual influx of seaweed from the beds off Bognor Regis, torn up by the summer storms and Atlantic currents and dumped on the beach.

Local people are known as Worthingites.

Town's nickname: Sunny Worthing, first coined by Emmanuel Rodocanachi – a Greek banker who settled in West Worthing around 1897 – to celebrate Worthing becoming top in the nation's sunshine league. The slogan was first used by the borough in the early 1900s.

It is the largest town in West Sussex.

In 1963 Post Office cancellation: 'At the foot of the South Downs – Sunny Worthing.'

In 2005 Worthing became Fairtrade, making a commitment to support, and use products bearing the trademark.

Grid Reference

Ordnance Survey grid reference: TQ 148029.

Worthing Town Hall, Chapel Street, BN11 1HA was erected at a cost of £175,000, from a winning design by architect Charles Cowles-Voysey and was opened in May 1933 by Prince George, later Duke of Kent. The building is one of Worthing's many listed buildings.

CHARLES COWLES-VOYSEY
F.R.I.B.A.
IN AN OPEN ARCHITECTURAL
COMPETITION ✦ DESIGNED
THIS ELEGANT TOWN HALL

OPENED BY HIS ROYAL HIGHNESS
THE PRINCE GEORGE
K.G., G.C.V.O.
22ND MAY 1933

Street Names

Ann Street (1807) – Named after Edward Ogle's wife, Worthing's leading citizen of the day. It was also the home of the Theatre Royal; Thomas Trotter's cottage (actor and manager); the market; the infirmary; and the police station. It became a public highway in 1809.   Today only the south side remains since the Guildbourne Centre and car park were built in 1968–1972.

Essenhigh Drive – Named after Flight Officer E.G. Essenhigh whose 49 Squadron Lancaster crashed on Worthing Beach in 1944. Other streets named after the crew members include: Varey Road; Bourne Close; Moore Close; Rees Close; Thomson Close; and Callon Close.

Montague Street – Originally Cross or West Lane and led to village of Heene. At one time it boasted seven inns, three chapels and two halls. It was pedestrianised in 1968, and is now one of the main shopping streets.

Ophir Road – Named after the ship of the same name that ran aground in 1896.

Rowlands Road – A corruption from rough lands (fields).

Swandean Corner – Known as Steer's Bank, infamous for highway robberies.

Winton Place – Known as Bo-Peep Lane until 1889 because of its association with smugglers.

Warwick Street – Originally part of Old Worthing Street.

Lost Streets:
Gloucester Place – Formally Pusses Croft, between Nos 86-88 Montague Street, demolished in 1964–1965 for Graham Road car park.

Kings Row – Lane named from a Preventive Officer post, at the north end of Paragon Street, now the multi-storey car park east of Augusta House.

ANN STREET T

ESSENHIGH DRIVE

OPHIR ROAD

Number Crunching

13 – Number of wards in the Borough: Gaisford, Salvington, Broadwater, Central, Tarring, Goring, Castle, Selden, Marine, Heene, Offington, Durrington, Northbrook.

37 – Number of councillors which represent the thirteen wards.

700 – This bus will take you from Worthing to Southsea (west) and from Worthing to Brighton (east).

3,000 – Number of jobs created by tourists every year.

01903 – Telephone area code for Worthing.

44,128 – Number of households in the Borough (2012).

5,300 – Number of children between the ages of 0–4 years living in Worthing. (2,700 are male, 2,600 female.)

2,550,722 – Number of passengers that passed in and out of Worthing station (2010–2011)

BN11, BN12, BB13, BN14, BN99 – postcodes for Worthing.

107.7 – Local radio, Splash FM.

23 – Number of primary schools in the Borough.

6 – Number of secondary schools in the Borough.

2 – Number of colleges for Further Education.

360 – Hectares of park and open spaces in the Borough.

43,800 – Employee jobs in the Borough.

38,900 (88 per cent) – jobs in the service sector.

5 – Railway stations: East Worthing, Worthing, West Worthing, Durrington-on-Sea and Goring-by-Sea.

53,000 – Number of day trippers that visited Worthing on August Bank Holiday 1935.

Demographics

The population of Worthing in July 2010 was 100,200.

White	94.8%
Asian	2.1%
Mixed race	1.3%
Black	0.9%
Chinese and other	0.9%

Car ownership is lowest in the Central ward, which also has greatest number of homes rented from a private landlord (30.6 per cent).

Offington ward has the highest percentage of detached homes.

Heene and Central wards have a high percentage of flats, 74.2 per cent and 60.1 per cent respectively.

Anti-social behaviour is higher in Central ward, but levels didn't increase from 2009–2010.

Total crime in Worthing decreased by 15 per cent for the period September–November 2009, and burglary rates across the wards were low, although there was a marked increase in the Salvington ward for the period September–November 2009.

Distance From ...

	Miles	Km
Ayers Rock, Australia	9,352.65	1,5050.02
Brussels, Belgium	206.38	332.13
Centre of the Earth	4,573.74	7,360.72
Death Valley, USA	5,295.17	8,521.76
Eiffel Tower, Paris	180.34	290.23
Frankfurt, Germany	401.43	646.04
Glasgow, Scotland	383.92	617.86
Hong, Kong, China	6,014.16	9,678.85
Istanbul, Turkey	1,553.30	2,499.80
Jerusalem, Israel	2,236.75	3,599.70
The Kremlin, Russia	1,586.32	2,552.94
Lima, Peru	6,302.81	1,0143.39
Mumbai India	4,483.89	7,216.12
Niagara Falls, North America	3,573.64	5,751.22
Osaka, Japan	5,954.38	9,582.64
Panama Canal, Republic of Panama	5,273.03	8,486.13
Queenstown, New Zealand	1,1804.94	1,8998.21
Reykjavik, Iceland	1,208.19	1,944.39
Syracuse, Sicily	1,224.29	1,970.30
The Taj Mahal, India	4,300.27	6,920.61
Ural Mountains, Russia	2,314.44	3724.73
Vatican City, Italy	866.64	1,394.72
Washington DC, USA	3,674.39	5,913.18
Xanthi, Greece	1,377.07	2,216.18
Yellow Stone National Park, USA	4,503.86	7,248.26
Zurich, Switzerland	468.44	753.89

Twinnings

The first twinning took place in May 1997 with the Black Forest, Elztal region in south-western Germany. The region includes the towns Waldkirch, famous for the manufacture of fairground organs, and Elzach, on the river Elz, 26km north-west of Freiburg, and the villages Gutach and Simonswald in the district of Emmendingen, Baden-Württemberg.

The second twinning took place in October 1998, with Le Pays des Olonnes.

The area consists of Olonne sur Mer, Château d'Olonne and the well-known French seaside resort of Les Sables d'Olonne ('the sands of Olonne') in the Vendée region, situated on the Atlantic coast.

Other Worthings

There are surprisingly few Worthings around the world.

The nearest is the small village of Worthing in Norfolk, approximately 26 miles from Kings Lynn.

Worthing, Texas, 4 miles west of Hallettsville in Central Lavaca County, USA, was named after A.H Worthing who built a store to serve the local farmers. With the decline of cotton planting in the 1950s business diminished. By 1987 the business had gone, and the population has remained static at fifty-five (2000).

Worthing in Lincoln County, South Dakota, USA, is on the wild-west plains where Native Americans fought the US Cavalry. It was first settled in 1871, when the prairies that teemed with buffalo were converted into a vast corn belt.

Worthing Beach, Barbados, is located on the southern coast, just 5km from Bridgetown, and boasts ten hours of sunshine a day.

Development of the Town

The area was first settled 5,000 years ago by Neolithic man extracting flint at Cissbury Ring.

The remains of Bronze Age habitation, dating back 3,000 years, have been found in the town.

The village became part of a 'grain' factory in fifth-century Roman times.

During the Saxon period the village became a fishing hamlet and agricultural area, remaining so until the late eighteenth century.

1750s – The first visitors arrived, when it was believed that bathing in seawater could heal.

1798 – Princess Amelia visited and the town developed into a seaside resort, a preferred alternative to Brighton for the wealthy and genteel.

1803 – An Act of Parliament formed a body of men called Commissioners to clean up and pave the streets, and it became a town.

1811 – *The Times* recorded that the Georgian resort was 'crowded with fashionable visitors during August and September.'

1835 – The Old Town Hall opened on land given by Sir Timothy Shelley, father of the poet. The building served as a council chamber, jail, exhibition hall, fire station and seasonal court.

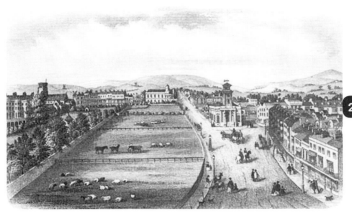

1845 – The railway opened between Worthing and Shoreham.

Worthing's sunny position made market gardening the town's major industry for a century

1890 – It was made a borough, and the population reached 16,000.

1893 – A typhoid epidemic affected around 2,000 and killed 188 people.

1908 – The museum and art gallery was built.

1921 – The population reached 35,000.

1939 – Worthing flourished as a seaside town, and the population reached 67,000.

1939–1945 – Forty-four people were killed in air raids, and ninety-seven houses were destroyed.

1968 – The Aquarena opened.

1974 – Many old buildings were destroyed to make way for the Guildbourne Shopping Centre, including two important buildings, the Theatre Royal and Omega Cottage.

2000 – The millennium garden at Highdown opened.

2011 –The Splash Point area of the town underwent regeneration.

2013 – The Splash Point swimming pool and fitness centre opened.

Seafaring

Fishing – Worthing has been a fishing village since at least the sixteenth century, the main catch being mackerel and herring, sold locally or exported to other towns.

Smuggling – Fishermen supplemented their income by plundering wrecked ships and smuggling illicit contraband, the flat beach at Goring being a favourite haunt. When cargo was landed, dozens of men helped as speed was essential as was delivery of the goods to local hostelries with no questions asked. The downlands behind Goring were famous for flocks of sheep, however it was not the fleece that was smuggled out, but live sheep, no doubt interesting to watch. In 1832 300 kegs of contraband French brandy, Dutch gin and perfume were unloaded opposite the Steyne. Excise Officers gave chase and one smuggler, William Cowerson, was shot and thirteen taken prisoner. Ferring resident John Olliver, a miller and reputed smuggler, built himself a coffin thirty-six years before his death, kept on castors under his bed. Legend claims that the coffin was used to store smuggled goods, and the blades of his windmill set to inform smugglers that it was safe to unload.

Disasters – In November 1850 eleven local men lost their lives going to the aid of the *Lalla Rookh*, leaving nine widows and forty-seven children fatherless. The tragedy led to the inhabitants subscribing for the town's first lifeboat, which came into service in 1853. In another incident in November 1894, a ferry boat went to the aid of a steamer carrying coal from South Wales that was in distress during a hurricane storm. A sole survivor was spotted in a lifeboat, but within metres of the shore the boat flipped, and he drowned. During the course of the day all the bodies were washed ashore. One body was repatriated to South Wales and the reminder, including two unidentified, were buried in a mass grave in the town's cemetery.

Curiosities – Many of the fishing family surnames start with the letter B: Belton, Belville, Blann, Bashford, Burgess and Brownrigg. Today the fishing families still keep a boat on the beach to retain their right to trade and fish.

Historical Timeline

Saxon invaders found village of Worthing.

Princess Amelia visits Worthing.

A market charter granted to West Tarring.

St Paul's Chapel of Ease is built

Flint mines are worked at Cissbury.

BC *C.* 3600   *c.* 450   1444   1798   1812

c. 210   1086   1643   1803

A Roman Villa and bath are built on Highdown.

Durrington chapel is attacked by the Parliamentarians.

Worthing is recorded in the Domesday Book with a population of twenty-two.

Worthing becomes a town.

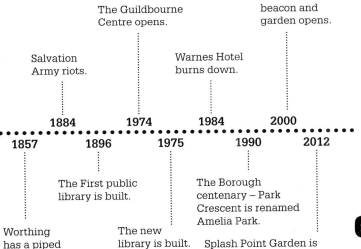

Salvation Army riots.

The Guildbourne Centre opens.

Warnes Hotel burns down.

Millennium beacon and garden opens.

1884   **1974**   **1984**   **2000**

1857   **1896**   **1975**   **1990**   **2012**

The First public library is built.

The new library is built.

The Borough centenary – Park Crescent is renamed Amelia Park.

Worthing has a piped water supply.

Splash Point Garden is dedicated to lifeboat crew and fishermen who manned the boats between 1850 and 1930.

29

Flora and Fauna

There is an abundance of wild flora and fauna in and around Worthing. Here are a few spotted during the year.

Wild flowers

Red dead nettle, wild daffodils, groundsel, stone crop, sandwort, celandine poppy, garlic mustard, wild cress

Birds

Common seagulls, green woodpeckers, jay, collared doves, greenfinches

Animals

Squirrel, fox

Butterflies

Speckled wood, orange spot, tortoiseshell, chalk blue

Little-Known Facts

60,000 gas masks and 168,000 sandbags were distributed during the Second World War.

The town had three lending libraries in 1831: the Apollo, named after the sun god and patron of poetry and music; Mrs Spooner's Colonnade, and Stafford's.

The average house price in Worthing (Jan–March 2012) was £212,170; flat, £148,807; terrace house, £185,605; semi-detached, £234,994; and detached, £322,392.

The Mayor's chain, bought in 1891 by public subscription, weighs 32oz, is 24ct gold and is insured for £215,000.

At the age of sixteen, Angela Barnwell reached the final of the women's 100m freestyle in the 1952 Helsinki Games, despite being knocked down by a tram four days before competing.

Harry Hill was a locum at Worthing Hospital before becoming a comedian. He made his first appearance at the Pavilion Theatre in 1995.

Katie Price, the glamour model, owns a house in Goring-by-Sea.

Cucumbers were exported to the mines in South Wales, and used by miners to quench their thirst.

Broadwater Green once housed a Ducking Pond, not to drown witches, but as a punishment for local misdeeds and spreading gossip, as depicted in the sign on the Broadwater pub, hand-painted by the local sign painter Nick Hallard.

During the Second World War the Raili Family Vault at Broadwater and Worthing Cemetery was used to hold Worthing's Council papers.

Beach inspectors patrol the beach, foreshore and promenade four times a day in the summer and once a day in the winter, on quad bikes, to check the pier and safety equipment situated along the promenade. In summer they also patrol the shoreline from Ferring to Lancing in two Tornado 5.3 rigid-hull inflatable boats.

The Broadwater

Most Iconic Building

The Dome

In 1911 the Kursaal was opened by Swiss entrepreneur Carl A. Seebold (actor and theatre manager). It was one of the first multi-entertainment centres in the country offering roller-skating, a dance hall, billiards, and a tearoom. The name is German, and means a building offering a health resort and entertainment under one roof in seaside and spa towns. Because of anti-German feeling in the town during the First World War, it was renamed the Dome. In 1922 it was converted into a cinema, and opened with *Pollyanna*, starring Mary Pickford. In 1970 Worthing Borough Council took over the building with the aim of demolishing it to build a shopping complex, but the 'Save the Dome' group rescued it, and it has now been taken over by the Worthing Dome and Regeneration Trust, and is a listed building. It closed in 2005 to undergo a £2.5m refurbishment, made possible by one of the largest grants awarded in Sussex from the Heritage Lottery Fund, £1.654 million, with English Heritage contributing £250,000.

Today, besides the regular film programme, there is a monthly Monday Club, with a performance for teenagers and adults with special needs, a Silver Screen performance on the last Wednesday of the month, with a mix of classic and modern films, and a Saturday morning children's film performance.

Entertainment

1796 – A Barn Theatre existed.

1807 – The 700-seated Theatre Royal opened with a performance of *The Merchant of Venice*.

1883 – Thanks to a gift by Sir Robert Loder, the New Theatre Royal opened in Bath Place. The main hall was converted into a 1,000-seat theatre in 1897 and reopened with a performance of *As you Like it*.

1916 – Connaught Hall and Theatre opened on the upper floor of Connaught buildings, Union Place, with stage and vaudeville entertainment provided. The Ritz Digital, seen today, is the original theatre. Digital 3D projection was installed in 2010, and films can be enjoyed by 242 people at a time.

1926 – The Pier Pavilion, designed by Adshead & Ramsey in a German 'kursaal' style, opened as part of the seafront improvements, and is mainly used for concerts, variety and pantomime. The 850-seat auditorium was modified in 1981–1982, and the exterior extensively refurbished.

At the same time a band enclosure (now the Lido) was opened with a canopy over the stage. The circular dome shelter seen today dates from 1929.

1931 – Walter Lindsay obtained a licence and the Connaught Theatre was launched, with its Art Deco façade. Today it presents first-class plays and musicals throughout the year, as well as one of Worthing's two pantomimes.

1934 – The Assembly Halls opened. Now a Grade II listed building, it was designed by C. Cowles Voysey in Art Deco style. It houses the largest Wurlitzer in Europe, opened in 1981 after an extensive restoration programme lasting five years, and regularly features in BBC radio broadcasts. It holds 930 people and ten wheelchairs for concerts, and 1,100 for standing concerts.

AMC Leisure on the seafront, formally called Connaught Leisure, contains three floors of entertainment.

The Pier

The wooden decked pier is 960ft (292m) long and 36ft (11m) wide and was originally constructed as a landing stage. Paddle steamers, the most famous being the *Worthing Belle*, regularly moored on the southern end of the pier, as does the more recent *Waverley* and the *Balmoral*.

The first pile was driven into the seabed in July 1861 and the pier, designed by Sir Robert Rawlinson, was made up of ninety-six girders, 3,791 planks, 3,122 bolts and 15,660 nails. It cost £6,500 and was officially opened in April 1862, with the pier chairman's daughter first through the turnstile.

It was renovated in 1887 to mark Queen Victoria's Diamond Jubilee.

In March 1913 a violent Easter storm destroyed the deck, leaving the pier a wreck of tangled girders. The southern end became completely detached and was nicknamed Easter Island.

In March 1921 Worthing Borough Council purchased the pier for £1,897.15*s* and, after renovations, visitors were charged 2*d*.

Disaster struck again in September 1933 when fire destroyed the south pavilion. Once again it was refurbished and remodelled. When it reopened in 1935 it was dubbed the 'suntrap of the south' by the *Daily Mirror*. In 1940, as a step to hinder the threat of a German invasion after Dunkirk, a 120ft hole was deliberately blown in the decking near the south pavilion. Two years later, as threats lessened, the pier became a recreation area for troops and included a canteen, library and billiard tables. After the war, the hole was repaired though a grant from the Government War Damage Commission and the pier reopened to the public in April 1949.

In 2006 it was awarded the title 'Pier of The Year' by the National Press Society.

To celebrate its 150th anniversary in 2012, a party was held on the pier, with the *Worthing Journal* commissioning a 5ft-long cake. Today the south-end pavilion is currently empty, but will hopefully soon be occupied.

Buildings

In Worthing there are over 360 listed buildings, including three Grade Is, although many old buildings were lost during rebuilding in the 1960s.

The Old Palace Tarring – When West Tarring was given to Canterbury by King Athelstan, King of England (924-939), it is likely that the bishops had an establishment here, because the building is traditionally known as the Palace of the Archbishops of Canterbury. The flint and stone building seen today is a thirteenth-century house with a fifteenth-century hall that was converted into a rectory at the time of the Reformation. When the new rectory was built the original building became a parish hall, and thanks to a grant from the Historic Buildings Council in 1958, it was restored.

St Mary's Parish Church, Broadwater – This church was mentioned in the 1086 Domesday Book and was once a parish in its own right before being incorporated into the Borough of Worthing in 1902. Little of the Saxon building remains, but work carried out in 1939 revealed a Saxon doorway. The Normans built a small church of which only the tower remains, and legend informs us that there is a Norman tunnel leading from the church to the nearby Broadwater Manor School, believed to have been used as a smuggling route. When Jane Austen visited the town and stayed at Stanford Cottage, off Warwick Street, she worshipped at the church.

Castle Goring – This is an interesting building because it is not a castle, or in Goring. It was built between 1797 and 1825 by Shelley's grandfather, Sir Bysshe Shelley, in the far north of the borough, and contains two distinct styles of architecture. The front south side of the building, in Palladian style, is yellow bricked and was designed by John Biagio Rebecca; it is said to be a copy of a villa near Rome. The north Gothic-style side is said to resemble Arundel Castle, 8km to the west. In 1845 Mary Shelley inherited the building and sold it to the Somerset family. Sadly the future for Castle Goring looks bleak as it has been left to decay and is now on the English Heritage's list of neglected buildings.

Other Buildings

Medieval – There is a late fifteenth-century row of cottages, the oldest dwellings in the borough, in Parsonage Row, Tarring.

Regency – There are so many fine Regency buildings, such as Park Crescent, once one of the most fashionable areas in Worthing. The three-storey stuccoed houses were built by Amon Henry Wilds, the famous Regency architect of Brighton. The ambitious project included a 'Triumphal Arch', now the entrance to the Crescent, but financial problems prevented the Crescent from being completed.

Ambrose Place (1810–1826) – This was named after Ambrose Cartwright, one of the contractors who built the terrace and lived at No. 14, which was later the home of Harold Pinter. The front gardens are on the opposite side of the road to allow the residents to bring their horse and carriage closer to the front door in bad weather.

Beach House, also called Marino Mansion – This was designed by John Rebecca and built around 1820 for Robert Carey Elwes. It was later owned by the Loder family, notable benefactors of the town, and guests included Edward VII, in 1908 and 1909. In 1917 the American playwright Edward Knoblauch (Knoblock) bought the house and employed Maxell Ayrton to make improvements. His many guests included Arnold Bennett, J.B. Priestly and Compton Mackenzie. In 1937 the Council bought the property and it was used as offices and to accommodate Spanish Civil War refugees. It is now in residential use.

Liverpool Terrace – To commemorate the Earl of Liverpool, this terrace was built between 1814 and 1826 by Henry Cotton. These elegant bow-fronted houses once overlooked a small, gated Pleasure Garden with a bowling green and archery.

There are a few remaining buildings in High Street dating to the late nineteenth century, although the cobbled-fronted cottage (No. 44) may be older.

Inside and Out

The outside of the Art Deco Connaught Theatre, and the inside of one of the theatre dressing rooms.

The West Cornwall Pasty Co., South Street, opened as the Ship Grill in 1933 and had portholes along the inside walls, partially filled with water, and at the touch of a switch a wave motion was created, a most unusual feature in its day. The impressive building was built from local timber by local craftsmen at the Tower Joinery Works, Warwick Street.

At the back of Savers in Montague Street, still in situ, is the church window of the Independent Congregational Chapel that once occupied this site. The 1804 building pre-dated St Paul's Anglican church, and was rebuilt by local architect Charles Hide.

Iconic Building of Yesteryear

Warnes Hotel

George Hilbery Warne (1864–1916) founded his hotel in 1899 in part of York Terrace on Marine Parade and it became Worthing's leading hotel. He was an early motoring enthusiast, and promoted his hotel as the 'Motorists' Mecca', establishing in 1900 the first hotel/garage breakdown service, a forerunner to the RAC in England. In 1902 he organised a trial run between Crystal Palace and Worthing with lunch served at the hotel for around 250 competitors, before returning via Arundel.

It is claimed that the first association for motorists, the Motor Union, was founded here in 1903. The hotel became a limited company in 1915, the year before he died. In 1928 cocktail bars and lounges were added, and in 1932 it was completely redecorated and refurbished, its seventy-five bedrooms each being given a telephone, hot and cold water, a gas or electric fire, and access via a lift to all floors. Over the years there were many famous visitors to the hotel including King Edward VII, King George V, Prince George of Kent, Winston Churchill, General Montgomery, General Eisenhower and the writer T.S. Eliot. Emperor Haile Salassie of Ethiopia and his family lived in a suite in the hotel after being forced from their homeland by Italian Fascists in 1936. In 1947 the garage was demolished. With the advent of cheaper air travel, holidaying on the south coast declined and in 1985 the hotel closed. Two years later a serious fire destroyed the building and it was demolished, being replaced by a new block of luxury apartments.

DONATED BY ROFFEY HOMES LIMITED

IN 1899

GEORGE WARNE
1864-1916

AN EARLY MOTORING ENTHUSIAST
PROMOTED HIS NEW HOTEL AS

THE MOTORISTS' MECCA

ESTABLISHING THE FIRST HOTEL GARAGE,
OR ENGINE HOUSE, IN ENGLAND
ON THIS SITE IN YORK ROAD IN 1900

THE GARAGE WAS DEMOLISHED
IN 1947

THE WORTHING SOCIETY 2006

Almshouses and Charity

Humphrys Almhouses were founded in 1858 by Robert and Ann Humphreys in memory of their son Harry. They were to be occupied by Anglican married couples, widows or spinsters resident in the parish of Broadwater. Six houses were built and two more followed in Portland Road in 1867. The will of Jane Butler (1936) bequeathed £100 to buy cigarettes and tea for the inmates, and in the 1960s the income was distributed at Christmas. The Butler bequest was amalgamated with the almshouse charity in 1972, and today is managed by the Humphrys Almshouse Charity.

The Elizabeth Almshouses in Clifton Road were founded in 1859 by Alfred Burges of Blackheath (Kent). He gave £650 to build houses for four women, preferably members of the Church of England, and £1,700 in stock as an endowment and to pay weekly allowances. The two-storey building is distinctive becasue of its red brick with two bands of grey headers and stone dressings. By 1864 the founder had increased the endowment to £2,260 stock, and in 1915 the endowment had increased to £3,800 stock.

In 1880 the Worthing and Broadwater Provident & Relief Society began in Grafton Road to provide coal in winter and run a soup kitchen, but it was not formally opened until 1892. In 1893, during the typhoid outbreak, the kitchen opened every day. On the roof of the building is a terracotta figure standing clutching a jug, which may symbolise the distribution of soup in bygone days. Affectionately known as the Lady of Provident House, she has a tale to tell. Sometime in the 1960s a local man threw a cooking apple at the statuette and she lost her arm. Three decades later, a chance conversation led to another man mentioning that he found the hand holding a bowl lying on the pavement and that the pieces were in his shed. With the help of Worthing Borough Council's conservation officer, work began to repair the statuette, and thanks to the skills of a Worthing potter the arm was reconnected and a new thumb made. It was unveiled in May 1992 by the mayor to celebrate the centenary of the town's oldest soup kitchen.

Planning Disasters

Grand Avenue was laid out in 1887 as part of the West Worthing development and imposing plans were passed in 1893 for a 370-room Hotel Metropole, together with plans for a second pier. However, soon after the Dutch gabled facade was complete, the developers ran out of money and the empty shell stood idle, becoming known as 'Worthing's White Elephant.' It was finally completed as flats in 1923 and named Grand Avenue Mansion, then Dolphin Towers in 1924, and finally, since 1971, has been known as Dolphin Court. A modern block of flats now occupies the south face.

A more recent 'disaster' in the eyes of local Worthingites is the Guildbourne Centre in the heart of the town. It was built in the 1960s when a great deal of historic architecture was destroyed, including the Old Town Hall (1968), Theatre Royal and Omega Cottage (1970), and Heene Manor (1971) to name just a few.

Around the same time Worthing saw the development of several car parks at Broadwater Bridge, Griffin House and Grafton Road, as well as out-of-character buildings such as those in Shelley Road and Marine Parade, plus the Aquarena Complex and commercial developments on the Lyons Farm Estate.

Events

Flingathon – Worthing beach

May Day Morris Dancers' Procession – Steyne Gardens

Three Forts Marathon (27.2 miles) taking in the ancient hill forts of Cissbury Ring, Devil's Dyke and Chanctonbury Ring

Broadwater Cemetery Tours running from May to October – South Farm Road

Worthing Rowing Regatta

May Bough Procession and Morris Dancing – Tarring High Street

Worthing Open Houses

The Big Open Kitesurfing

Queen Alexandra Hospital Home Open Day

Sunny Worthing Weekend

Race for Life

Worthing Lions Festival

Beer Festival – Henty Arms

Steven's Fun Fair

Splash FM Garden Party

Goldwing Motorcycles, Bus Rally and American and Custom Cars

Dragon Boat Race

England Men's and Mixed National Bowls Championships

International Birdman Festival

Worthing Carnival

Pier Day

Findon Sheep Fair and Village Festival

Boxing Day Dip in the Sea

In the Limelight

1898 – Several early films were made by William Kennedy Laurie Dickson, the father of film-making, including *Water Polo, Launching the Life-Boat: Coming Ashore*, and *Worthing Life-Saving Station*.

1968 – *Up the Junction*, starring Suzy Kendall, Dennis Waterman, Adrienne Posta, Maureen Lipman and Liz Fraser, showed shots of Dennis Waterman driving along the promenade to give the appearance he was driving along the open road. It tells the story of a 'well-to-do' becoming friends with a couple of girls, and a planned dirty weekend at a hotel in Marine Parade, now the Travelodge.

1968 – The film version of Harold Pinter's play *The Birthday Party* was filmed opposite Heene Terrace on the seafront.

1987 – *Wish You Were Here*, starring Emily Lloyd and Tom Bell, centred around the town, most notably the Dome. It is set in the 1950s and is believed to have been based on the early life of Miss Whiplash (Cynthia Payne), born in Bognor Regis.

1995 – The film *Dance with a Stranger* starring Miranda Richardson was partly filmed on Worthing beach.

1998 – An episode of the sitcom *Men Behaving Badly*, titled 'Gary in Love' and starring Martin Clunes and Neil Morrissey, was partially filmed at the Eardley Hotel, called Groyne Hotel in the film. The hotel has been replaced by thirty-four luxury seafront apartments overlooking Splash Point.

2012 – The film *Sea Monsters*, directed by Julian Kerridge and starring Rita Tushingham, was filmed at the Lido, the Pier and Brooklands Pleasure Park.

Notable People

Edward Snewin (1813–1900) and **Henfrey Smail** (1909–1979) were two notable people who did much to preserve the history of the town. Edward Snewin lived most of his life in Worthing, and in 1898 wrote a descriptive account of life in the nineteenth century. Henfrey, in his day, was the town's leading historian and based his research on the material collected by the Snewin family; he published a series of books on the town.

Alfred Cortis (1833–1912) was elected to the local Board of Health in 1881. In 1890 he was chosen to be the first Mayor of the new Borough Council. He was a generous benefactor to the town, funding a new drinking-water supply following the typhoid epidemic, and secretly donating £5,000 towards the building of Worthing's Museum & Art Gallery.

Ellen Chapman JP (1847–1925) was the first female councillor, alderman, and magistrate. She became the first female mayor and was elected twice in 1920–1922. Although first nominated in 1914, she was not elected as it was considered unwise to select a woman at war time.

Horace Duke, 'The Duke' (1924–1995), was a familiar sight around Worthing from the 1960s, becoming an ambassador for the town. He was an elegant eccentric, inspired by his visits to the Brighton Hippodrome and the dress of Max Miller. He could be seen riding around the town on a bicycle or a motorbike, upright and well mannered, dressed in topper, bowler, or boater and tweeds or blazer, much to the amusement of passers-by. When he died, his coffin, in a glass-sided hearse, was pulled by two black horses.

William Robert Ames, '**Bubbles**' (1877–1952), became a well-known character as he collected for charity in front of St Paul's church, Chapel Street. No one was sure how he acquired his nickname but some say it was earned as a boy. Before the First World War he worked on the estate of King Edward VII, before joining the Norfolk Regiment. He was wounded three times and ended up in a spinal chair. In 1932, he came to live in Gifford House (Queen Alexander Hospital Home).

Museum, Art Gallery and Library

Worthing Museum & Art Gallery – The building was partly financed by the Scottish philanthropist Andrew Carnegie and local benefactor Alfred Cortis, and started life as the library. Today it has one of the largest collections of costumes and toys in the country, including a pair of Princess Amelia's shoes and a cloak and undergarments belonging to Queen Victoria. The art gallery offers an interesting programme of contemporary and historical exhibitions, and there is a sculpture garden.

Worthing Library – The library was opened in 1975 and was designed by RIBA (Royal Institute of British Architects) Frank C. M. Morris, who in 1977 was presented with a RIBA award for his design. The well-stocked library also houses an excellent local study centre.

Employers

Market Gardeners – In 1814 three market gardeners operated in Worthing: Head's in Anchor Lane (now Lyndhurst Road), Jordan's, and Long's. Others followed, Frampton's, Kempshott Vineries, Ashwood's, A.G. Linfield, Ladydell and Barnwells, to name a few. Worthing became known as the birthplace of large-scale gardening when John Head erected the first glasshouses, after recognising that the climate and brick earth soil was suited to producing early fruit and vegetables; business flourished for over a century. The pioneers of large-scale glasshouses were a Broadwater company, C.A. Eliot, who purchased glass from the Great Exhibition in 1851 to build them, and by 1899 the area as known as the 'town of hot houses'. By the early 1900s the area was known for its grapes, cucumbers, tomatoes, strawberries, mushrooms and chrysanthemums; in fact, 600 tonnes of produce were exported to places as far afield as Leeds, Manchester and Glasgow. Durrington became an important lavender-growing district. Robert Piper being the most extensive grower with 105 glasshouses, whilst A.G. Lingfield had a main crop of mushrooms and peppers. In 1931, 1,513 male agricultural workers were employed in market gardening, and during the Second World War most flower production was replaced by food crops, with tomato production reaching its peak in the 1940s. Although glasshouse production remained the main industry, much land was sold for resident housing.

Tourism – This has been a thriving industry since the arrival of Princess Amelia in 1798, and in 1955 55,000 visitors were recorded as staying in the town between May and September. In addition, more than 50,000 visitors came on a day's outing, generating £1.5 million for the local economy. Today there is still a healthy tourism business and 266,776 people stayed in Worthing in 2010, staying a total of 982.761 nights, an average of 3.8 nights each, and spent a total of £57,051,613. Also 1,901,473 day visitors came to the town and between them spent £61,969,016, making a total of £119,022,000 visitor spend that year.

Famous for ...

Tomatoes

The aroma of seaweed

Macaris ice cream

The headquarters of English bowls

Sunshine

A continual programme of events throughout the summer months

The pier

Theatre entertainment

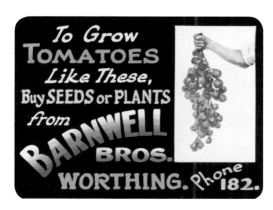

To Grow **TOMATOES** *Like These*, Buy SEEDS or PLANTS *from* **BARNWELL** BROS. WORTHING. Phone 182.

Infamous for ...

Worthing's resident 'down and outs' that congregate around the Liverpool Gardens area

Seagulls, especially one with a sweet tooth, who steals chocolates from Thorntons

Oscar Wilde and his infamous court case in spring 1895

Traffic jams

Poor parking facilities

Splash Point

Splash Point, 300m east of the pier, was so named because currents caused the waves to break on the seafront, providing a spectacle for those who gathered. During the Second World War it was the site of a large gun, and was where people, mostly evacuees, congregated for daily beach services. Boulders have been heaped on the beach to reduce the force of the waves, making it a more tranquil place to visit, especially after its 2012 facelift. Local artists Marina Burgess and Tone Holmen created some of the images engraved on slate boulders, each depicting a story from the town's history: the Highdown Goblet made around 400 BC and discovered in 1827; Knuckerholes and Knucker Dragons; the town's connection with the Rosetta Stone; Oscar Wilde; and Worthing's fishing and horticulture industries. Splash Point is also the name of the new £17.5 million swimming pool and fitness centre; the name was jointly chosen by two sisters who won a year's Fit4 membership worth over £500, in a competition to name the pool. It will replace the Aquarena when it opens in 2013.

Literary Connections

John Selden (1548–1654) – a legal antiquary, jurist and politician born in Salvington. In his honour the area around Francombe Road was once known as Seldenville.

Percy Bysshe Shelley (1792–1822) – Shelley's first two works, *Original Poetry by Victor and Cazire* (1810) which he wrote with his sister Elizabeth, and *The Necessity of Atheism* (1811) written with his friend Thomas Jefferson Hogg, were printed by C.W. Phillips in Warwick Street.

Jane Austen (1775–1817) – Her unfinished novel *Sanditon*, based on a fictionsal south-coast seaside resort, is said to have been inspired by her visit to Worthing in 1805.

John Oxenham (1852– 1941) Born William Arthur Dunkerley, he moved to Worthing in 1922. He wrote under both names, but used John Oxenham for his poetry, hymn-writing, and novels.

Elsie Jeanette Dunkerley (1880–1960) – A children's writer who took her father's name, Oxenham (as above), as her pseudonym. Her first book, *Goblin Island*, was published in 1907. She is best known for her Abbey series. Two further titles, discovered in the 1990s, have since been published by her niece.

Oscar Wilde (1856–1900) – His play, *The Importance of Being Ernest*, includes the character Mr Worthing. It was written in a room he rented at The Haven, No. 5 Esplanade in 1894. The building has since been demolished and replaced by a block of flats and a garage; the only visible sign is a blue plaque on the wall.

Richard Jefferies (1848–1887) – An author and naturalist who spent the last ten months of his life living in Sea View, Goring. It has now been named Jefferies House to commemorate his brief stay.

James Bateman FRS (1811–1897) – An orchid specialist who published *Orchidaceae of Mexico and Guatemala*. He lived in Francombe Road where he constructed an alpine garden.

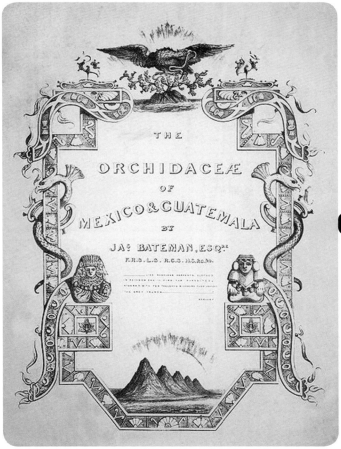

THE

ORCHIDACEÆ

OF

MEXICO & GUATEMALA

BY

JAS. BATEMAN, ESQR.

F.R.S. L.S. R.G.S. H.S. &c. &c.

What They Said

1820 – 'Worthing is a handsome and fashionable watering and sea-bathing place, frequented by those who prefer retirement and quiet to the hustle and dissipation of Brighton ...'

Pinnocks' History and Topography of Sussex

1883 – 'Worthing is a place which we shall not flatter ... but we can with perfect impartiality recommend it as possessing strong inducements of comfort and pleasure not always found in large places of resort.'

J.D. Parry, Historical and Descriptive Account of the Coast of Sussex

1965 – 'Worthing is an exasperating town. Put very briefly it began by imitating Brighton and ended by imitating Bournemouth ... the result is that architecturally it is full of brave beginnings and ignoble endings ... the most genteel of Sussex resorts without any of Bournemouth's compensations.'

Ian Nairn and Nikolaus Pevsner, *Buildings of Sussex 1965*

1999 – 'It's one of the finest places in Britain. It's a traditional quiet, peaceful seaside town. The people are nice, there is a good shopping centre and the seafront is splendid.'

Derek Jameson, resident; former editor of the *Daily Express*

2010 – 'An odd town, with a mix of 1970s nostalgia and history. There is plenty to suit all ages, dozens of summer events, and is full of friendly people, a true community spirit.'

Ben, a visitor to the town from Durham

2012 – 'Worthing suffered terribly at the hands of the planners in the 1950s and '60s, when much of the old town was swept away, being replaced by car parks and grim-looking shopping centres. However, the town can boast one of the south coast's finest piers and it enjoys 5 miles of coastline and the backdrop of the glorious South Downs. It is still a good place to live.'

Chris Hare, local historian

A Glimpse at a Few Churches

St Andrews, Tarring, is the oldest church in the area, and was built in the twelfth century. It is first mentioned in 1372 and remained a peculiar (exercised jurisdiction over the parish) of Canterbury until 1845. It is a large church which proves its medieval importance. Its 137ft-high spire was used during the Armada as a signalling station. The mosaic panels covering 200sq. m of the north, west and south walls of the nave are claimed to be one of the finest and largest mosaics in the country. They were designed by William Butterfield FSA (1814–1900) and were constructed in 1885. Conservation work began in 2005 and was completed in 2006. Another unusual feature is the misericords, sometimes called mercy seats, which have a folding shelf on the underside of a folding seat to provide comfort during long periods of prayer.

St Paul's church was built on the corner of Ambrose Place in 1812 as the Chapel of Ease because the Parish Church at Broadwater was too far and not big enough to accommodate the growing population. It became dilapidated but has been given a new lease of life as the Lime Café, and is home to several activities.

English Martyrs church has an impressive reproduction of the famous Sistine Chapel ceiling in Rome. It is two-thirds the size of the original, with brilliant colours that bring the images alive. Local artist Gary Bevans spent five years painting the reproduction, the only known replica outside Rome. It was completed in 1993.

Green Spaces and Parks

The borough contains 360 hectares of parks, open spaces and woodlands, including:

People's Park set out in Victorian times, now called Homefield Park

Denton Gardens created in 1924

Steyne – used for various events throughout the year, this becomes an ice rink during December–January

Brooklands Pleasure Park 'Diddyland' – paddling pool, trampolines, bouncy castle, pony rides, Diddy's miniature train rides

Beach House Park – home to Bowls England, it has a mix of trees, shrubs, and seasonal planting, and is also home to the pigeon memorial

Highdown Gardens – has a wide variety of plants and colour throughout the year, and hosts outdoor Shakespearean performances.

Children's Park – Marine Parade

Titnore Ancient Woods, formally part of the Castle Goring estate

Southdowns National Park – accessible from Worthing

Born, Lived or Died in Worthing

Born

Anthony Salvin (born 1799), an expert on medieval architecture, and an important figure in the Victorian Gothic Revival, learning his skills in the office of John Nash.

Maureen Duffy (born 1933), a contemporary poet, playwright and novelist who published a biography of Aphra Behn.

Britt Allcroft (born Hilary Mary Allcroft), best known for producing the TV series *Thomas the Tank Engine and Friends*.

Byron Dafoe (born in 1971), a British/Canadian former National Hockey League goaltender for the Washington Capitals.

Nicolette Sheridan (born 1963), an American television actress who starred in the soap *Knots Landing* (1986–1993) and *Desperate Housewives* (2004–2009).

Jonathan Cake (born 1967), an actor who worked on various TV series and who is best known as Jack Favell in *Rebecca* (1997) and *Oswald Mosley* (1997) and for films such as *Brideshead Revisited* (2008) and *Krews* (2010)

Lived

Jessie Bond, a singer and actress with the D'Oyly Carte Opera Company who moved to Worthing in the 1920s, best known for her mezzo soprano soubrette roles in Gilbert & Sullivan comic operas.

Alexandra Bastedo (1946–), an actress, model and animal lover lived in Sea Place. She starred as Nemesis agent Sharron Macready in the 1960s cult TV series *The Champions*. She also appeared in *The Saint*, *Randall and Hopkirk (Deceased)*, *The Adventurer*, *Jason King* and *Department S*.

Peter Bonetti (1941–), Chelsea and England goalkeeper. He moved to Worthing in 1948, and his parents ran a café on the seafront next to the Dome. He played for Worthing Football club.

Roxanne McKee, an actress in Hollyoaks, grew up in Worthing and attended Our Lady of Sion School.

Alma Cogan (1932–1966), a singer, had a number of hits in the 1950s and become one of Britain's highest paid singers. Her father owned a tailor's shop in the town.

Tony Caunter, Roy Evans in Eastenders, attended Worthing High School.

Bob Monkhouse moved here in 1939 and attended school at Goring.

Died

Edward William Lane (1849–1876), an Arabic scholar and author of *Manners and Customs of the Modern Egyptians*, and translator of *The Thousand and One Nights,* who died in Union Place.

Peter Tuddenham, an actor, best known for his roles in cult dramas *Blake 7* and *Doctor Who*. He moved to Worthing in 1961 and lived here until his death in 2007.

Elsie Jeanette Dunkerley, a children's author, died in Worthing in 1960, aged seventy-nine.

Hugh Lloyd, an English actor, best known for his appearances in *Hugh and I* and other 1960s sitcoms, died at his home in 2008.

Walter Dew, a police officer involved in the hunt for Jack the Ripper and Dr Crippen, died in 1947 and is buried in Durrington Cemetery.

Blue Plaques

Edward Knoblock – Playwright. He lived in Beach House 1917–1923.

Percy Bysshe Shelley – Poet and radical thinker. Two of his earliest works were printed in Warwick Street.

King Edward VII – Stayed in Beach House in 1907, 1908, 1909 and 1910.

Oscar Wilde – Stayed at Esplanade Court.

Private William Cooper – Lived in Cranmore Road and fought in the Boer War at Rorke's Drift in 1879 against the Zulus.

Worthing's Soup Kitchen – A replacement plaque was erected on Provident House in Grafton Road. The Soup Kitchen has played a significant role in the town's social history.

Harold Pinter (1930–2008) – Playwright, actor and director. He lived at No. 14 Ambrose Place with his wife Vivien Merchant (1962–1964) where he wrote one of his best known plays, *The Homecoming.*

Jane Austen – Stayed at Stanford Cottage.

EDWARD KNOBLOCK
(1874 – 1945)

PLAYWRIGHT OF
"KISMET"

LIVED IN
BEACH HOUSE
1917 – 1923

KING EDWARD VII
(1841 – 1910)

STAYED IN
BEACH HOUSE
1907 – 1908 – 1909
& 1910

HAROLD
PINTER
1930 - 2008

PLAYWRIGHT
ACTOR AND DIRECTOR

LIVED HERE
1962 TO 1964

THE WORTHING SOCIETY 2009

JANE AUSTEN
1775 - 1817
NOVELIST
STAYED HERE AT
STANFORD COTTAGE
FROM 18TH SEPTEMBER 1805
TO THE YEAR END

THE WORTHING SOCIETY 2010

The Unusual, the Unique

Numerous Twittens – narrow paths between houses, walls or hedges, that connect passages such as Steyne Passage, Field Row and Chapel Fields, used by smugglers and as a short cut home during blackouts in the Second World War.

Boat porches – a feature unique to Worthing, derived from the days when fishermen used their upturned boat as shelters in bad weather.

Tarring Folly – built in 1893 in the garden of solicitor Mr W. Boyes, as a study and place to escape from his wife and daughters.

Worthing Journal, published by Paul Holden, records history as it happens and also the quirky side of Worthing, providing vital information on events, new venues and entertainment in the town.

Broadwater and Worthing Cemetery

The Friends of Broadwater and Worthing Cemetery was formed to revive and preserve some of the 26,000 graves which had fallen into disrepair and to restore the cemetery back to its former glory as an idyllic place of rest. The Friends acquired a £30,000 Heritage Lottery Grant in 2008 and organise regular tours between May and October on a variety of themes: Seafarers, Worthing Mayors, Shopkeepers and the Typhoid Epidemic. They aim to give visitors an insight into the lives of past residents. Each tour has an accompanying booklet that visitors can buy.

One of the many interesting graves is that of Mary Hughes who was the actual Mary of the nursery rhyme 'Mary had a Little Lamb', and died aged ninety-one. Either Sarah Hale or Miss Buel (it is not certain) penned the rhyme while staying on the Hughes Farm at Llangollen after she watched a lamb following Mary. A lamb is cut into the simple headstone.

IN
Ever Loving Memory of
OUR DEAR MOTHER
MARY HUGHES,
WHO PASSED AWAY DEC 9TH 1934
IN HER 61ST YEAR
HEROINE OF THE NURSERY RHYME
Mary had a little lamb
At Rest.

Home at last my journey done
Safe and blessed the victory won
Jesus passed from pains set free
Jesus now has welcomed me
ALSO
In Memory of
JULIA V. MEDLICOTT
DIED 14TH FEBRUARY 19
Peace, Perfect peace

The Unexplained

Why Molly Corbett is buried in Worthing remains a total mystery. Born in 1912, she died in Lausanne, Switzerland, at just fifteen years of age, in 1928. Her fitting memorial, the finest in the cemetery, depicts a statue of Our Lady of Grace, head bowed, hands outstretched, but records her age as sixteen. The burial records state that Molly was buried in the vault beneath the memorial, sixteen months after her death. From the burial records we learn that her father Maxwell Campbell Corbett, a mining engineer, died in Mexico City and was buried with his daughter in June 1947, some thirty months after his death. Molly's mother, Eileen Kathleen Veronica Corbett (*née* Reid), died in Brisbane, Australia, in May 1985 and, like her daughter and husband, is buried in the family vault. Grave diggers at the time reported that the vault is fully tiled and that Molly is interred in a glass coffin. To date, the Friends of Broadwater and Worthing Cemetery have failed to find any connection between the wealthy family and Worthing, so the mystery remains unexplained, for now.

Crowds

Historical Crowd
Queen Victoria's Diamond Jubilee Celebration in the People Park, now Homefield Park.

Modern Crowd
Watching the Dragon Boat Race at Brooklands Pleasure Park, 2012.

Secret Worthing

Salt may have been extracted at Worthing in 1219.

Around 1871 Chaplin Brothers of No. 4 Montague Street produced a 'Worthing Sauce' in glass bottles, at 1s 6d. It was used with fish, game, chops, steak and cold meats, and contained two unique ingredients, one of which aided digestion.

The ornate fountain gracing Gaisford Close once formed part of the extensive grounds of Woodside, built during the late 1920s/early 1930s, and was the home of local pre-war property developer Percy Brazier. The fountain formed the focal point of the putting green, with a large garden, open to the public. Gaisford Close was built in the 1970s in the grounds of Woodside and the fountain was kept in situ.

In 1912 a horse-drawn coach service began between Arundel and Brighton, the horses being changed at West Tarring.

In 1814 Thomas Young came for his annual holiday, bringing with him a copy of the Rosetta Stone inscriptions. He worked on them and was able to show that some of the hieroglyphs on the stone deciphered the Royal name of Ptolemy. The French scholar Jean-François Champollion realised that the hieroglyphs recorded the sounds of the Egyptian language and, as they say, the rest is history.

Tucked away off Second Avenue is 5.33 acres called Charmandean Open Space, an enclosed informal park with a small central copse of ash and beech trees, given as a gift to the Borough Council by Frank Sandell & Sons in 1937.

After the Second World War, the red-brick Maybridge estate, planned by Charles Cowles-Voysey, was built between 1948 and 1956, by prisoners of war.

Pamela Brooks (1921–2003), a naval decoder in the famous 'Hut 13' at Bletchley Park during the Second World War, lived in Ferring.

War Memorials

The Second Boer War memorial at the south end of the Steyne was unveiled in August 1903 by Maj.-Gen. Sir H.M. Leslie Rundle, and commemorates the twenty-six local men killed in the Second Boer War (1899–1902).

A large stone cross outside St Paul's church in Chapel Street contains ninety-eight names engraved on a plinth, commemorating parishioners who lost their lives in the First World War.

The Cross of Sacrifice in Broadwater and Worthing cemetery. This is usually present in cemeteries containing forty or more war graves. On the face of the cross, designed by Sir Reginald Broomfield for the Commonwealth War Grave Commission, is a bronze sword, blade down, representing a resting place of military personnel.

The Town Memorial in Chapel Street was moved to its present position at the corner of Chapel Street and Stoke Abbot Road when the Town Hall was built. The bronze figure in military dress on a stone pedestal was erected by Francis Tate, and was unveiled in April 1921 by Field Marshal Sir William Robertson. The original list of 660 was increased by 342 after the Second World War.

Britain's only war memorial dedicated to the pigeons who carried messages, explosives and other items to secret destinations during the Second World War was erected in Beach House Park. It was the brainchild of local actress and playwright Nancy Price who, with members of the People's Theatre in London, commissioned the memorial that was designed by local sculptor Leslie Sharp and unveiled in 1951. It consists of a circular mound, planted with shrubs, and a rockery with streams and pools of water. The stones, quarried in the Forest of Dean, were refurbished in 1999, and the memorial is maintained by the Borough Council.

Folklore and Traditions

In January the ancient custom of wassailing takes place in Tarring to bless the apple trees. A torchlight procession proceeds down Tarring High Street where people gather around an apple tree to shout, chant, and sing to ward off the evil spirits. The trees are toasted with wassail, cider apple and apple cake, followed by a firework display.

On May Day, a procession and dancing takes place in Worthing town centre, culminating in the crowning of the May Queen.

Legend informs us that on Midsummer's Eve skeletons would rise up from the roots of Broadwater's Midsummer tree, and dance around the tree at midnight. Local historian Chris Hare and friends keep alive the tradition and dance around the tree.

John Olliver, a reputed smuggler, died in 1793. Legend says that if you run around his tomb twelve times at midnight, his ghost will jump out of the tomb and chase you.

According to legend, a tunnel stretched from the now demolished Offington Hall to the Neolithic flint mines and Iron Age Fort at Cissbury, where treasure was buried. At some time the tunnel had been sealed off, and despite several attempts to locate it, all have been driven back by snakes, said to be guarding the treasure, springing out with open mouths.

Knucker is a type of wingless water Dragon rumoured to live in the bottomless ponds called 'Knuckerholes'. One of these was believed to be located by Ham Bridge, near East Worthing station and the Teville stream.

Cafés

There are numerous cafés for shoppers and visitors to rest and enjoy good food.

The most famous café is the Sea Lane café where you can enjoy a drink and relax, but be prepared to queue as it is always busy.

The Warwick Street 'hub' of bars and cafés, again, is busy, especially on a sunny day at lunchtime.

The Sunny Café at Splash Point

The Bluebird Café at Ferring is very popular with walkers and dog lovers. There is a list of 'doggie laws' which read, 'If you are: Well behaved/On a lead/Friendly/ You're welcome'.

Feast sandwich shop in Warwick Street is the newest café in town. Town planners ordered the owners to remove the giant mural above the shop, fearing it would set a precedent in an historic town, but the owners have appealed, and so for now the colourful mural can stay for six months.

Sport

Worthing Football Club (formed in 1886) is the town's main football club and plays in the Ryman's Isthmian league, Division 1 South. They were once called the Mackerel Men, a reference to the local fishing industry represented on the club crest. The club's intriguing present nickname, the Rebels, dates from when they resigned from the West Sussex League over a rule change, prior to becoming a founder member of the Sussex County League.

Worthing United Football Club was formed in 1988, and are nicknamed the Mavericks. They play in the first division of the Sussex County League.

Worthing & District Harriers The first Harriers were active in the 1860s and the present Worthing Harriers began a connection with Brighton in 1921, becoming a separate group in 1927. Claire Moyle, coach for the Worthing Harriers Special Olympics Group, received the honour of carrying the Olympic Torch.

Worthing Rugby Football Club, established in 1920, started when a group of sportsmen met at York House. They had no ground or equipment and borrowed a field from a local farmer before moving to the Rotary Ground at Broadwater, with the Cricketers Arms used for changing! In 1977 the club moved to its present location in Angmering, which includes six pitches, two of which are floodlit, and, with the aid of a lottery grant, established Women's Rugby. They are nicknamed the Raiders and play in the National League 2 South.

Worthing Cricket Club was established in 1855 and play home games in the Sussex Premier League at Manor Sports Ground.

Worthing's Basketball team – Worthing Thunder – were formed in 1999 and play in the English Basketball League.

M's Cycle Hire is situated on the promenade, south of Steyne Gardens.

Worthing is the Home of Bowls England National Bowls Championships held each August at Beach House Park, well known for its velvet lawns.

Riotous and Rebellious

Worthing's Bonfire Boys – During the nineteenth century Guy Fawkes Night was traditionally a night for protests and demonstrations, not unique to Worthing. In 1852 a mob of Bonfire Boys with blackened faces, staves, and blazing tar barrels rampaged out of control. The following year Archbishop Cardinal Wiseman's effigy was burnt, and in 1877 violent riots resulted in a confrontation with the police. By 1880 the 'Worthing Bonfire Club' was launched, later to become the 'Worthing Excelsior Bonfire Club', in honour of Longfellow's heroic poem.

Skeleton Army – When the Salvation Army arrived in the town in 1883, the Bonfire Club changed its name to Excelsior Skeleton Army, and sought to oust the Salvationists. In 1884 troops were called upon to quell the unrest when the army's 'barracks' in Prospect Place and the Hall in Montague Street were destroyed.

In more recent times, there was a return of the riotous spirit of the Bonfire Boys when large crowds of youths, mainly Teddy Boys, confronted the police on Guy Fawkes Night in 1959, throwing bricks and bottles and setting fire to shops. Many arrests were made.

Rebel extraordinaire – Patricia Baring (1895–1981) moved to Worthing in 1963 and quickly became a leading conservationist, strongly opposing insensitive development of the town. In 1973 she founded the Worthing Civic Society, and in 1975, at the age of eighty-two, saved the Victorian lamp post at the junction of Church Walk and Francombe Road from destruction by sitting in the path of a pneumatic drill. The lamp post, the only one of its kind in Worthing, is now a Grade II listed building of special architectural and historic interest. In 1979 she fought to save Bedford Row from demolition, and was largely responsible for saving Beach House from being demolished in 1980.

Visit The Lavender Lady

FOR

MORNING COFFEE
LIGHT LUNCHES
AFTERNOON TEA
HOME MADE
CAKES & BREAD

(Near Steyne Gardens) **35 Brighton Road**

Advertisements from Yesteryear

WALTER BROS. LTD

The Worthing Mart

58 & 60 MONTAGUE ST.

and at TARRING

GENERAL
DRAPERS
FURNISHERS
Boys' and Gent's
OUTFITTERS

Linoleums, Blinds &
General Housefitting

ALL BEST MAKES IN
TENNIS RACKETS AT
STORE PRICES

*Specialists in Fancy
Materials for Ladies'
Jumpers*

Telephone
152

Our Outside Pinoleum Blind is "Sunny Worthing's Most Delightful Shade"

DRAPERY BAZAAR, 2, 4 & 6 South St.

NOTED HOUSE FOR SPORTS GOODS

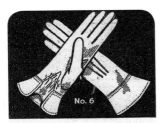

Statues and Sculptures

The Desert Quartet, the Montague Centre, Liverpool Gardens – This is a series of four large heads created by Dame Elisabeth Frink (1920–1993) who, with Henry Moore and Barbara Hepworth, is considered to be one of the greatest British sculptors of the twentieth century. The heads were completed in 1989 and were so called because they were inspired by feelings she had whilst in the Tunisian desert.

The Winged Horse, pavilion roundabout – The Worthing Town Centre Initiative recently installed a plinth on the replanted pavilion roundabout, and has offered local artists the chance to display sculptures in the town. Alan Tobias-Williams' piece, The Winged Horse, was selected as the first 'Sculpture by the Sea'. He has cut and worked with mild steel for twenty years. The piece was chosen because of its links with flying and the Worthing International Birdman competition.

The bronze bust of James Gurney Denton JP (1857–1937) by Miss S.I. Nichols (1930) is displayed in the Assembly Hall and a smaller version is in the Denton Lounge. Denton Garden, situated east of the pier, was presented to the town in 1922 by Alderman Denton, and was opened in spring 1924. Towards the end of his life, Mr Denton donated the then huge sum of £40,000 (about £2 million today) for the building and furnishing of the Assembly Hall. The Denton Lounge was opened in 1959 using the remaining money from his bequest.

The Promenade

A rough path along the seafront from West Buildings to Warwick Road was turned into a promenade during 1819–1821 and named the Esplanade.

As the town's popularity grew it was extended in 1865 to Heene Road, and by the 1930s it was further extended to Wallace Avenue and George V Avenue, becoming known as West Parade. East of Warwick Road became Beach Parade, then from New Parade to the Brighton Road, the Esplanade. Known for its bracing air, its numerous annual events, and 5 miles of coastline, today it is used by residents and visitors alike.

Along the Shore

Oranges and Lemons – In March 1901 the residents must have thought it was their lucky day when cases of oranges and lemons came ashore and littered the beach. The SS *Indiana* was sailing to London from Venice via Valencia with the citrus cargo when she hit thick fog and collided with another ship, *The Washington*. A tug came to her rescue, but whilst in tow she listed heavily and finally ran aground 1 mile south of Worthing pier. The crew were taken to Newhaven, and eventually the cargo of oranges and lemons were washed ashore as far as Goring in the west and Rottingdean in the east. Large quantities of fruit were pick from destruction ed by local residents and stallholders and, by the time the salvage boat arrived, the beach was clean. The *Indiana* became known as the 'Orange Wreck', and an information board detailing the incident can be seen near Worthing pier. To mark the sinking of the ship, an annual orange and lemon 'flingathon', is held in March on the beach. Fruit is kindly donated by Waitrose and contestants pay £1 for a throw, with the proceeds going to a local charity.

Surrounded by Wood – In 2008 a different cargo was swept onto the beach: 2,000 tonnes of wood. It was washed ashore at Worthing and Ferring from a Greek-registered ship, *Ice Prince*, heading for Egypt, that sank 26 miles off the Dorset coast. This time the beach was closed to sightseers to allow heavy machinery to remove the wood. In 2009 a stained-glass window, created by local artist Chris Brown, was unveiled on Worthing pier, and Worthing Arts Council organised an 'Ice Prince Festival' to mark the first anniversary of the shipwreck.

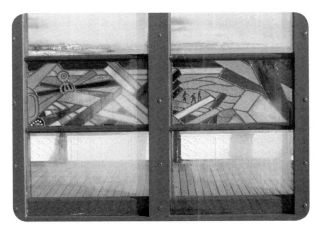

Worthing Saved

On 17 December 1944, a 49 Squadron Lancaster bound for Munich, loaded with bombs and incendiaries, encountered mechanical problems. Unable to ditch the bombs, the crew realised that they were over the town of Worthing and, looking for safety, saw that the tide was out. They turned seaward and attempted to land on the beach wheels up, but off Heene Terrace they hit a wartime defence and the plane immediately exploded, sending flames high into the sky. Sadly all seven crewmen were killed. They were: Flight Officer Edward Gordon Essenhigh (pilot), aged twenty-four; Sgt Harry Varey (flight engineer), aged twenty-four; Sgt Leonard Bertie Bourne (navigator), aged twenty-eight; Sgt Fredrick Bernard Rees (wireless operator), aged twenty-two; Sgt James Worral Moore (mid-upper gunner) aged thirty-nine; and Flight Officer James Andrew Thomson (bomb aimer), aged twenty-five. The body of Sgt Gordon Frederick Callon (rear gunner), aged twenty, was the only one recovered, and he is buried in Littlehampton. The rest of the crew are remembered on the Runnymede memorial in Surrey. In 2004 a memorial was unveiled by Mayor Cllr E. Mardell, and is situated on Worthing pier's ninth column.

Pilot	F/O E.G. Essenhigh
Flight Engineer	Sgt. H. Varey
Navigator	Sgt. L.B. Bourne
Wireless Operator	Sgt. F.B. Rees
Mid Upper Gunner	Sgt. J.W. Moore
Bomb Aimer	F/O. J.A. Thomson
Rear Gunner	Sgt. G.F. Callon

On the 17 December 1944 at 1930hrs., 49 Squadron Lancaster, fully loaded with high explosive bombs and incendiaries, was losing height because of mechanical problems. Unable to ditch the bombs for it would have blown its tail off, the crew looking for something soft and level to land on saw a beach - the tide being out.

It was pitch dark when the crew realised suddenly that they were over Worthing Town. Turning sharply seaward, and with insufficient height to make more than one attempt, landed on the beach, wheels up, hit a wartime beach defence and immediately exploded killing all the crew. Only one body was ever recovered, that of Sgt Callon. The only casualties in Worthing were some smashed windows.

Remember these brave men - they gave all their tomorrows for your todays.

Unveiled by the
Mayor Cllr E Mardell.
2002.

A Town Celebrates

2012 Jubilee and Olympic Celebrations

A–Z of Worthing

A – Amelia, Princess (1783–1810), youngest daughter of George III. Her arrival to convalesce from a knee infection in July 1798 marked the beginning of Worthing's status as a fashionable resort. When she left in December, she gave £20 to be distributed amongst the poor at Broadwater. As part of the Borough's Centenary celebrations in 1990, an inscription was erected in Park Crescent and the grounds were named Amelia Park.

B – Basque children. In 1937, sixty children from war-ravaged Bilbao arrived at the Beach House, after fleeing the Spanish Civil War. Local dairymen provided 8 gallons of milk a day, the Worthing & West Sussex Grocers' Association donated a minimum of 2 guineas of grocery a week, and the Bakers' Association supplied bread for less than the cost to make. Weekly collections were made by local employees and churches, and the children were cared for by people working a rota.

C – Cooks Row, which once housed Worthing's earliest Jail – the Black Hole.

D – Douglas Motorbike – the passion of Hilda Booth, one of the town's rebels who fought a lengthy public battle with the Council who refused to give her a taxi licence on the grounds that it was 'not an appropriate occupation for a woman'. However, her application was granted and she became Worthing's first female taxi driver.

E – Elegant – Regency houses around the town.

F – Figs. Legend states that Thomas à Beckett introduced figs to Tarring. From the Old Palace cuttings, an orchard was established in 1745, and by 1830 over 2,000 figs were being produced. The garden became a tourist attraction from 1875–1936, advertising a postal delivery service of ripe figs, but by 1987 the trees were destroyed to make way for development.

G – Gardner, Walter, who became the town's best known portrait and commercial photographer, and moved his business to No. 13–15 Royal Arcade in 1925. Many of Walter's photographs can be seen at Worthing library.

BEACH HOUSE

In 1937 Beach House provided sanctuary for 60 refugee children from the Basque region of Spain who came to Britain fleeing bombing and starvation after the destruction of Guernica during the Spanish Civil War. They were supported and cared for entirely by local volunteers.

H – Henry Harris, a partner in Maynard & Harris, a naval and military outfitter. He left money for a rescue craft, and in 1887 Worthing's new lifeboat, *The Henry Harris*, was named after him.

I – Ivy Arch Studios, home to Worthing Sunshine local community radio, which caters for all musical tastes – jazz, soul, reggae and rock.

J – Jupps Barn, built by farmer George Jupp in 1771, adjacent to the English Martyrs church in Goring and used as a church hall today.

K – Kim's Bookshop, No. 7–11 Chatsworth Road, which sells new, second-hand and antiquarian books.

L – *Lalla Rookh*, Worthing's greatest tragedy. Most of the men who died were acting as volunteer rescuers in the absence of a lifeboat service. Residents and civic leaders raised £5,000 for the families. At the Cavendish Hotel can be found the Lalla Rookh Restaurant.

M – Mitchell, Horace, English cricketer (1858–1951). A right-handed batsman who made his debut for Sussex against the Marylebone Cricket Club in 1882, he next appeared for Sussex in the 1891 County Championship against Lancashire. He died in the village at West Tarring where he was born.

N – Nostalgic town.

O – Octav Botnar (1913–1998), or OB to his staff, was a self-made businessman and philanthropist. He lived in Worthing during the 1970s and ran an automobile import business, Datsun, known as Nissan UK since 1981. It was the first company in Britain to import Japanese cars.

P – Punch and Judy. Paul Pelman and Steve Gawley performed on the seafront from 1965–1976. Steve lived in Tarring Road and gave private indoor performances around the town. There was also a pitch east of the pier used by Robert Grey (Bert Donn), the Music Hall artiste, in the 1960s, and 'Uncle Charlie' gave shows in Beach House Park around 1948–1954.

Lalla Rookh

Restaurant

Q – Quashetts. The marshy area north of Teville Stream, an ancient footpath from the top of the High Street, is called the Squashes or Sqashetts, the 'S' being dropped later.

R – Royal Arcade, built on the site of the Royal Sea House Hotel. It was given the prefix 'Royal' after Queen Adelaide, consort of King William IV, visited in 1849.

S – Salvington Windmill. The only mill to survive in the area, this windmill ceased working in 1897, but occasionally ground flour until 1914.

T – Thomas Trotter, manager of the Theatre Royal, lived in Omega Cottage in Ann Street. Thomas played a key role in putting Worthing on the map by attracting actors and patrons to the town.

U – Union Place – home of the Worthing Conservatives.

V – Viva Products, Rowland Road, which sells Mediterranean food products

W – Wardroper, Walter (1847–1908) and Henry (1845–1910). They were well-known theatre entertainers and impersonators in the Victorian era who toured the UK with their act. When Walter retired, he bought the Maltsters public house in Broadwater, now the Broadwater, and ran it from 1893–1896.

X – XL Design Consultants Ltd, Chatsworth Road, which is an advertising and graphic design company.

Y – Yellow bricks. Worthing has distinctive buildings made from yellow bricks produced from blue clay taken from Worthing Common, which existed south of the beach but is now submerged.

Z – *Zadne*. A seafaring disaster which happened in1894.

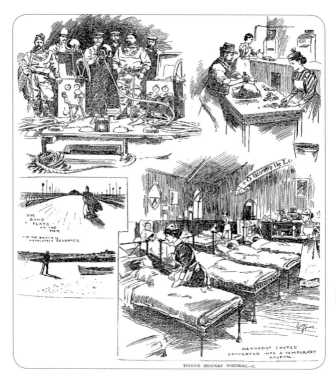

THE BAND PLAYS ON THE PIER

AND THE BEACH IS ABSOLUTELY DESERTED

METHODIST CHAPEL CONVERTED INTO A TEMPORARY HOSPITAL.

TYPHOID STRICKEN WORTHING.—II.

Websites

www.visitworthing.co.uk

www.worthing.gov.uk

www.worthingtowncentre.co.uk

www.worthingjournal.co.uk

http://oldworthingstreet.com

http://worthingpubs.com

www.worthingsunshineradio.co.uk

www.fbwc.co.uk

www.worthingfootballclub.co.uk

http://wpavilionbc.org

www.visitsouthdowns.com

www.worthingleisure.co.uk

www.m-cyclehire.co.uk

Things to Do in Worthing

Take a walk along the Promenade ☐

Visit the English Martyrs church at Goring ☐

Enjoy one or two of the many flavoured ice creams from Macaris on the seafront ☐

Visit the market in Montague Street on a Wednesday and pick up a bargain ☐

Sit on the beach on a warm summer's day ☐

Visit the Connaught Theatre to enjoy a play ☐

Eat an enormous breakfast at the Blue Bird café ☐

Watch the buskers in Montague Street ☐

Buy some fresh fish from one of the fishermen's stands ☐

Picture Credits

Unless otherwise stated, an image is not in need of credit.

Page:

2. Welcome to Worthing. (Conrad Hughes)

3. Town Coat of Arms – Worthing Town Centre Initiatives.

7. Aerial view Worthing 1980. (West Sussex Country Library Services www.westsussexpast.org.uk)

9. Town Hall and plaque. (Conrad Hughes)

11. Street signs. (Conrad Hughes)

17. Dome of the Rock, Brussels Town Hall, Taj Mahal, Vatican Dome of St Peter's. (Wikicommons)

19. Elzach, Le Sables d'Olonne. (Wikicommons)

21. Ernest & Young, Barbados. (Wikicommons)

23. South Street, 1816-17.

25. Montague Street, 2012. (Conrad Hughes)

27. Model of fisherman. (Conrad Hughes)

28/29. Cissbury Ring, Princess Amelia. (Wikicommons). Lifeboat memorial (Conrad Hughes)

31. Fox in cemetery. (Gail Spach, USA). Flower boat at Ferring. (Conrad Hughes)

33. Raili Mausoleum, Broadwater pub sign. (Conrad Hughes)

35. Dome being built. (West Sussex County Library Services, www.westsussexpast.org.uk); Dome today. (Conrad Hughes)

37. Band enclosure, 1953, Pier Pavilion today (Conrad Hughes)

39. Pier, 1889; children in front of pier, 1910; pier today. (Conrad Hughes)

41. Old Palace and Broadwater church. (Conrad Hughes)

43. Parsonage Row, Liverpool Terrace. (Conrad Hughes)

45. Cornish pasty shop, Connaught Theatre outside, dressing room. (Conrad Hughes)

47. Warnes, *c.* 1905. (West Sussex County Library Services, www.westsussexpast.org.uk); Motorists' Mecca plaque. (Conrad Hughes)

49. Elizabeth Almshouses. (Conrad Hughes)

51. Dolphin Court, Guildbourne Centre. (Conrad Hughes)

53. Race for Life, bus rally, carnival. (Conrad Hughes)

54. American custom cars; dragon boat race; fairground on the promenade. (Conrad Hughes)

55. Kitesurfing. (Conrad Hughes). Birdman competition. (Worthing Town Centre Initiatives)

57. Hotel used in *Up the Junction*. (Conrad Hughes)

59. Edward Snewin, Ellen Chapman. (Friends of Broadwater & Worthing cemetery). Horace Duke (*Worthing Herald*)

61. Museum & Art Gallery, library. (Conrad Hughes)

63. Market Gardeners (Malcolm Linfield, West Sussex Growers Association). GlaxoSmithKline (Conrad Hughes)

65. Tomatoes. (West Sussex Library Services, www.westsussexpast.org.uk). Seaweed; seagull. (Conrad Hughes)

67. Down and outs. (Conrad Hughes). Oscar Wilde. (Wikicommons)

69. Splash Point. (West Sussex Library Services, www.westsessex.org.uk). Splash Point today. (Conrad Hughes)

71. The Orchidaceae of Mexico & Guatemalia. (Wikicommons)

73. Derek Jameson. (Wikicommons). Chris Hare. (Chris Hare)

75. Misercords, St Andrews; Sistine chapel ceiling. (Conrad Hughes)

77. Homefield Park; Brooklands Park. (Conrad Hughes)

79. Alexandra Bastedo. (Alexandra Bastedo)

81. Jessie Bond. (Wikicommons)

83. Blue plaques. (Conrad Hughes)

85. Twitten Field Row; houses with boat porches; *Worthing Journal*. (Conrad Hughes)

87. Entrance to Broadwater and Worthing Cemetery; Mary Hughes. (Conrad Hughes)

89. Grave of Molly. (Conrad Hughes)

91. Queen Victoria's Diamond Jubilee at People's Park, 1897. (West Sussex Library Services, www.westsussexpast.org.uk); Crowd watching the dragon boat race, Brooklands Park, 2012. (Conrad Hughes)

93. Gaisford Close. (Conrad Hughes). Pamela Brooks. (*Worthing Herald*)

95. Pigeon memorial; town war memorial; Second Boer War memorial; Sword of Sacrifice. (Conrad Hughes)

97. Stomping Morris dancers; Midsummer Tree. (Conrad Hughes)

99. Sunny café, Splash Point; Bluebird café; Feast. (Conrad Hughes)

101. Worthing Harriers. (Worthing Harriers). Bowls.(Conrad Hughes)

103. Victorian lamp post. (Conrad Hughes). Riots.

104: Advertisements from yesteryear. (Various newspapers)

105. Advertisements from yesteryear. (Some defunct)

107: Dessert sculpture, winged horse; Splash Point sculptures. (Conrad Hughes)

109. Lido and promenade crowd. (Conrad Hughes). West Parade in 1914.

111. Fruit on beach. (West Sussex Library Services, www.westsussexpost.org.uk); Wood on beach. (Lynn McInroy); Stained-glass window. (Conrad Hughes)

113. Memorial on pier. (Conrad Hughes)

114. Olympic Torch; Party on Promenade. (Conrad Hughes)

115. Diamond Jubilee celebrations couple. (Conrad Hughes)

117. Beach House plaque. (Conrad Hughes); Hilda Booth. (*Worthing Herald*)

119. Lalla Rookh; Punch and Judy; Royal Arcade. (Conrad Hughes)

121. Thyroid epidemic; *Zadne* memorial. (Conrad Hughes)

123. Sunny Worthing. (Conrad Hughes)

125. Beach and Macaris. (Conrad Hughes)

128: Train at Worthing station. (Wikicommons)